MY FIRST BOOK ABOUT

IOWA

by Carole Marsh

This activity book has material which correlates with the Iowa Core Content for Assessment. At every opportunity, we have tried to relate information to the History and Social Science, English, Science, Math, Civics, Economics, and Computer Technology CCA directives. For additional information, go to our websites: **www.iowaexperience.com** or **www.gallopade.com**.

Coordinates with Iowa's™
Social Studies Curriculum

GALLOPADE INTERNATIONAL

Reading
Reference **R** **R** Research
R **R**
Reinforcement

Gallopade is proud to be a member of these educational organizations and associations:

SHOPA MEMBER™
School, Home, & Office Products Association

NSSEA

ASCD

The Iowa Experience Series

My First Pocket Guide to Iowa!

The Big Iowa Reproducible Activity Book

The Iowa Coloring Book!

Iowa "Jography!": A Fun Run Through Our State

Iowa Jeopardy: Answers & Questions About Our State

The Iowa Experience! Sticker Pack

The Iowa Experience! Poster/Map

Discover Iowa CD-ROM

Iowa "GEO" Bingo Game

Iowa "HISTO" Bingo Game

A Word... From the Author

Do you know when I think children should start learning about their very own state? When they're born! After all, even when you're a little baby, this is your state too! This is where you were born. Even if you move away, this will always be your "home state." And if you were not born here, but moved here—this is still your state as long as you live here.

We know people love their country. Most people are very patriotic. We fly the U.S. flag. We go to Fourth of July parades. But most people also love their state. Our state is like a mini-country to us. We care about its places and people and history and flowers and birds.

As a child, we learn about our little corner of the world. Our room. Our home. Our yard. Our street. Our neighborhood. Our town. Even our county.

But very soon, we realize that we are part of a group of neighbor towns that make up our great state! Our newspaper carries stories about our state. The TV news is about happenings in our state. Our state's sports teams are our favorites. We are proud of our state's main tourist attractions.

From a very young age, we are aware that we are a part of our state. This is where our parents pay taxes and vote and where we go to school. BUT, we usually do not get to study about our state until we are in school for a few years!

So, this book is an introduction to our great state. It's just for you right now. Why wait to learn about your very own state? It's an exciting place and reading about it now will give you a head start for that time when you "officially" study our state history! Enjoy,

Carole Marsh

Iowa
Let's Make Words!

Make as many words as you can from the letters in the words:

Iowa,
THE HAWKEYE STATE!

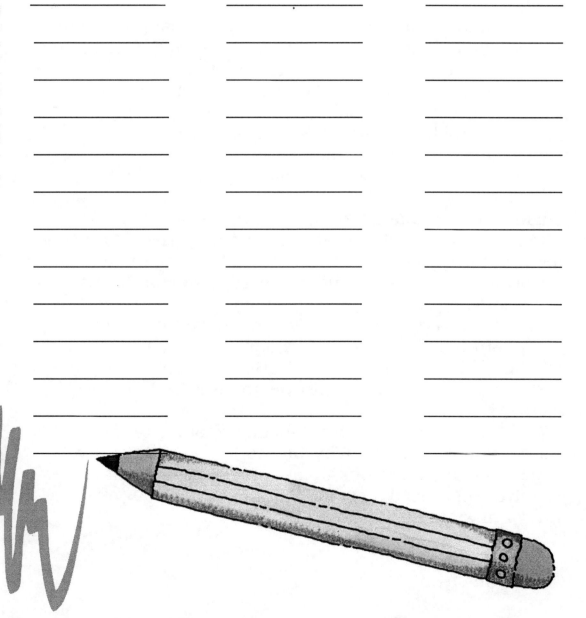

Iowa
The 29th State

Do you know when Iowa became a state? Iowa became the 29th state on December 28, 1846.

Color Iowa red. Color the Atlantic and the Pacific oceans blue. Color the rest of the United States shown here green.

Iowa
State Flag

Iowa's current state flag was adopted in 1921. It three vertical stripes that are blue, white, and red. An eagle with blue ribbons bearing the state motto appears on the white center.

Color Iowa's state flag below.

I pledge allegiance...

Iowa
State Bird

Most states have a state bird. It should remind us that we need to "fly high" to achieve our goals. The Iowa state bird is the eastern goldfinch. It is a colorful bird, and in summer, the male is bright yellow with a black head, wings, and tail. In winter, his coloring darkens. The female has a yellow breast and an olive-brown back.

Circle the Iowa state bird, then color all the birds.

The early bird gets the worm! *Yikes!*

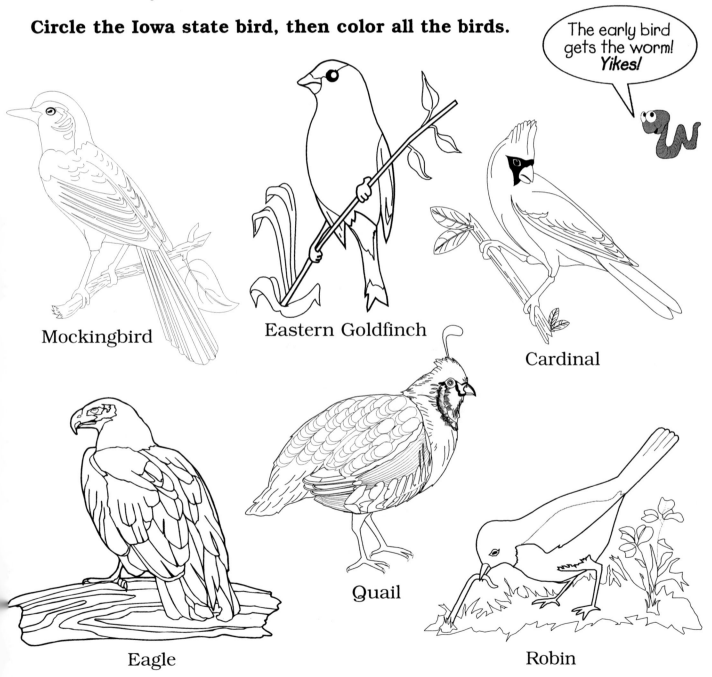

Mockingbird

Eastern Goldfinch

Cardinal

Eagle

Quail

Robin

Iowa
State Seal and Motto

Iowa's state motto is "Our liberties we prize, and our rights we will maintain."

In 25 words or less, explain what this motto means:

_____

_____

_____

_____

The state seal of Iowa shows a scene from the early days. A soldier stands in a wheat field, holding an American flag in his right hand and a gun in his left hand. The pictures of lead and a furnace stand for the state's industries. The plow, sickle, and rake represent farming. The Mississippi River is pictured in the background and an eagle flies overhead bearing the words of the state motto.

Color the state seal.

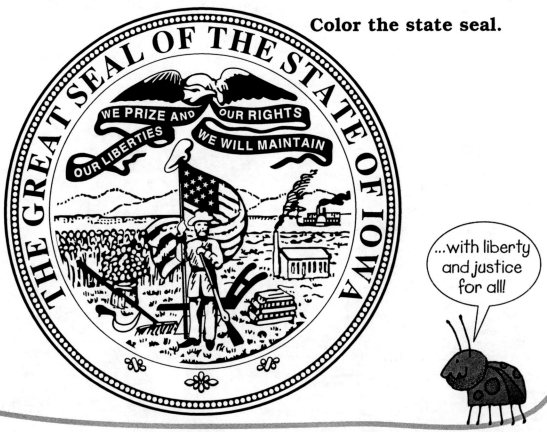

...with liberty and justice for all!

Iowa
State Flower

Every state has a favorite flower. The wild rose has been Iowa's state flower since 1897. Roses grow on small shrubs throughout the state and bloom in summer. Native Americans used the rose's leaves and stems for tea and medicine.

Color the pictures of the Iowa state flower.

Iowa
State Tree

The Iowa state tree reminds us that our roots should run deep if we want to grow straight and tall! Iowa's official state tree is the oak tree. Oak trees have green leaves with uneven edges; they turn color in fall.

Finish drawing the oak tree, then color it.

WOW!

Iowa State Zoo

Des Moines is home to the Blank Park Zoo. From big cats to reptiles, this zoo is a sight to see!

Match the name of the zoo animal with its picture.

Zebra

Giraffe

Chimpanzee

Bear

Tiger

Iowa
State Explorers

In 1673, Louis Jolliet, a French fur trader, and Father Jacques Marquette were the first two explorers to reach present-day Iowa.

Circle the things an explorer might have used.

Let's go exploring!

Iowa
State Rock

The geode is Iowa's state rock. It is found in limestone. Geodes are round and have an outer shell with an inside lining of mineral crystals. They are 2–6 inches (5–15 centimeters) around.

Put an X by each item that is not a geode and then color them all!

Iowa
One Day I Can Vote!

When you are 18 and register according to state laws, you can vote! So please do! Your vote counts!

Your friend is running for a class office.

Here is her opponent!

She gets 41 votes!

He gets 16 votes!

ANSWER THE FOLLOWING QUESTIONS:

1. Who won? ❑ friend ❑ opponent

2. How many votes were cast altogether?

3. How many votes did the winner win by?

Iowa
State Capital

Des Moines became the state capital of Iowa in 1857. There were two previous capital cities: Burlington and Iowa City. The current capitol building was completed in 1884.

Add your hometown to the Iowa map.
Now add these major cities:

Des Moines
Cedar Rapids
Davenport
Sioux City
Iowa City

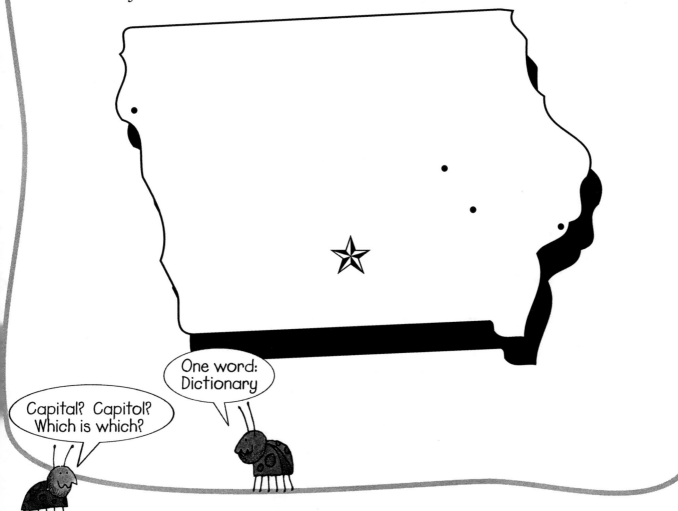

One word: Dictionary

Capital? Capitol? Which is which?

Iowa
Governor

The governor of Iowa is the state's leader.
Do some research to complete this biography of the governor.

Governor's name:

_____

Paste a picture of the
governor in the box.

The governor was born in
this state:

_____

The governor has been in office since:

_____

Names of the governor's family members:

_____
_____
_____

Interesting facts about the governor:

_____
_____
_____
_____
_____

Iowa
Crops

Some families in Iowa make their living from the land. Some of the state's crops or farm products are:

WORD BANK

Corn   Soybeans   Hogs

Sheep   Oats   Hay

UNSCRAMBLE THESE IMPORTANT STATE CROPS

yah _____

epesh _____

eabnsoys _____

hgso _____

taos _____

ronc _____

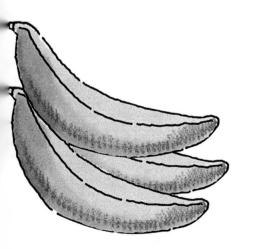

Iowa
State Holidays

These are just some of the holidays that Iowa celebrates.

Number these holidays in order from the beginning of the year.

Columbus Day 2nd Monday in October	Thanksgiving 4th Thursday in November	Presidents' Day 3rd Monday in February
Independence Day July 4	Labor Day first Monday in September	New Year's Day January 1
Memorial Day last Monday in May	Veterans Day November 11	Christmas December 25

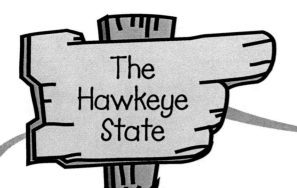

The Hawkeye State

Iowa
Nickname

Iowa has a very special nickname. It is called the Hawkeye State.

What other nicknames would suit Iowa and why?

_____

_____

_____

_____

What nicknames would suit your town or your school?

_____

_____

_____

_____

_____

What's your nickname?

Nick.

How BIG is the State?

Iowa ranks 26th in size in the United States. It has a total (land and water) area of 56,276 square miles (145,743 square kilometers).

Can you answer the following questions?

1. How many states are there in the United States?

_____

2. How many states are smaller than Iowa?

_____

3. How many states are larger than Iowa?

_____

Bigfoot was here!

ANSWERS: 1-50; 2-24; 3-25

Iowa
People

A state is not just towns, mountains, and rivers. A state is its people! Some really important people in a state are not always famous. You may know them—they may be your mom, your dad, or your teacher. The average, everyday person is the one who makes the state a good state. How? By working hard, by paying taxes, by voting, and by helping Iowa children grow up to be good state citizens!

Match each Iowa person with his or her accomplishment.

1. John Wayne

A. Famous actor of over 200 films

2. Johnny Carson

B. Newspaper columnist; writes advice column

3. William Frederick "Buffalo Bill" Cody

C. Longtime host of TV's *Tonight Show*

4. Ann Landers

D. Frontiersman, scout, and showman

5. Terry Branstad

E. Iowa's youngest and longest serving governor

ANSWERS: 1-A; 2-C; 3-D; 4-B; 5-E

Iowa
Gazetteer

A gazetteer is a list of places.

Use the word bank to complete the names of some of these famous places in Iowa:

1. Lewis and __ __ __ __ __ State Park

2. __ __ __ __ __ Madison

3. Blank Park __ __ __

4. Field of __ __ __ __ __ __ Baseball Diamond

5. Buffalo Bill __ __ __ __ Museum

WORD BANK

Clark   Fort
Cody   Zoo
Dreams

Iowa
Neighbors

No person or state lives alone. You have neighbors where you live. Sometimes they may be right next door. Other times, they may be way down the road. You live in the same neighborhood and are interested in what goes on there.

You have neighbors at school. The children who sit in front, beside, or behind you are your neighbors. You may share books. You might borrow a pencil. They might ask you to move so they can see the board better.

We have a lot in common with our state neighbors. Some of our land is alike. We share some history. We care about our part of the country. We share borders. Some of our people go there; some of their people come here. Most of the time we get along with our state neighbors. Even when we argue or disagree, it is a good idea for both of us to work it out. After all, states are not like people—they can't move away!

Use the color key to color Iowa and its neighbors.

Color Key:

Iowa-red
Missouri-yellow
Nebraska-dark green
South Dakota-orange
Minnesota-purple
Illinois-light green
Wisconsin-blue

Iowa
Highs and Lows

Iowa's highest point is Hawkeye Point in Osceoloa County. It rises 1,670 feet (meters) above sea level.

Draw a picture of a family having a picnic at Hawkeye Point.

The lowest point in Iowa is the Mississippi River at 480 feet (146 meters) above sea level.

Draw a picture of a boating scene on the Mississippi River.

Iowa
Old Man River

Iowa has many great rivers. Rivers give us water for our crops. Rivers are also water "highways." On these water highways travel crops, manufactured goods, people, and many other things—including children in tire tubes!

Here are some of Iowa's most important rivers:

- Mississippi River
- Missouri River
- Floyd River
- Little Sioux River
- Boyer River

Draw a kid "tubing" down the Missouri River!

Iowa
Weather... Or Not!

What kind of climate does Iowa have? Iowa's climate usually includes warm, moist summers and cold winters. Iowa's temperatures can drop to 6°F (14°C) in the winter and reach 86°F (30°C) in the summer.

You might think adults talk about the weather a lot. But Iowa weather is very important to the people of the state. Crops need water and sunshine. Weather can affect Iowa industries. Good weather can mean more money for the state. Bad weather can cause problems that cost money.

ACTIVITY: Do you watch the nightly news at your house? If you do, you might see the weather report. Tonight, turn on the weather report. The reporter talks about the state's regions, cities, towns, and neighboring states. Watching the weather report is a great way to learn about the state. It also helps you know what to wear to school tomorrow!

What is the weather outside now? Draw a picture.

Iowa
Indian Tribes

The American Indians were first on our land, long before it was a state. Some of Iowa's Indian tribes include:

Ioway	Illinois	Omaha
Missouri	Dakota (Sioux)	Winnebago

Help Maize find her way through the maize (corn) field maze to her hut made of saplings!

Start

Finish

Iowa
Website Page

Here is a website you can go to and learn more about Iowa:

www.50states.com

Design your own state website page on the computer screen below.

State Song

The official state song for Iowa is "Song of Iowa." Below is the first verse:

"Song of Iowa"
Words by S.H.M. Byers

You ask what land I love the best,
Iowa 'tis Iowa
The fairest state in all the west,
Iowa, O! Iowa
From yonder Mississippi's stream
To where Missouri's waters gleam,
O fair it is as poet's dream,
Iowa, Iowa, O! Iowa

How does the state song make you feel? Write verse about something in the state that means a lot to you.

_____

_____

_____

_____

_____

_____

_____

_____

_____

Iowa
State Fish

There are 149 different types of fish found in Iowa's rivers and lakes. The best time to catch some prize bluegills, crappies, and perch is in the winter. Iowa's frozen lakes are perfect for winter ice fishing.

Draw six fish in the water below. Color each one a different color.

Iowa
Spelling Bee!

What's All The Buzz About?

Here are some words related to Iowa.

See if you can find them in the Word Search below.

WORD LIST

STATE	RIVER	PEOPLE	TREE	BIRD
FLAG	VOTE	FLOWER	SONG	INSECT

```
A  X  N  Y  H  N  V  S  D  G  T  R  E  P
V  O  T  E  M  A  C  S  E  A  B  A  Y  E
S  N  B  R  X  B  R  K  S  X  B  D  S  O
Y  B  P  Q  L  S  O  N  G  R  I  J  H  P
R  I  V  E  R  P  P  L  R  T  Y  U  E  L
Q  R  E  R  R  Y  Z  E  E  R  T  O  N  E
R  D  P  P  A  E  A  O  N  E  C  K  A  R
S  X  O  C  E  A  W  C  T  C  E  S  N  I
P  O  B  U  Y  U  Y  O  E  O  L  L  D  O
Q  U  F  L  A  G  R  K  L  L  X  Z  O  P
Z  X  R  D  G  H  R  E  U  F  L  L  A  L
M  R  D  W  Q  N  M  N  S  T  A  T  E  Z
```

Iowa Trivia

I ♥ Iowa!

- Iowa ranks first in the nation in pork, corn, and soybean production.

- The first fast-food franchise was established in the 1920s in Muscatine: the Maid-Rite sandwich shop.

- The first microwave, the Radarange™, was introduced in Iowa in 1965.

- Iowa had the first woman dentist. In the 1865, Lucy Hobbs Taylor earned her Doctor of Dentistry degree.

- America's shortest railroad, the Fenelon Place Elevator, is in Dubuque.

- Many Amish live in Iowa. They live a simple life, driving horse drawn buggies, wearing plain clothing and work the land with horse-drawn plows.

- Cloid H. Smith was the first person to sell popcorn under a brand name, Jolly Time™. By 1938, there were three more major popcorn companies in Iowa, including Cracker Jack™.

Now add a fact you know about Iowa here:

_____

_____

_____

_____